KU-573-108

SURVIVE THE WORST AND AIM FOR THE BEST

Kerry Katona

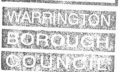 **SHORTLIST**

First published in 2007 by
Ebury Press
This Large Print edition published
2007 by BBC Audiobooks by
arrangement with
Ebury Press

ISBN 978 1 405 62216 5

Copyright © Kerry Katona 2007

Kerry Katona has asserted her right
to be identified as the author of this
work in accordance with the
Copyright, Designs and Patents Act
1988.

Quick Reads™ used under licence

British Library Cataloguing in Publication Data available

Printed and bound in Great Britain by
Antony Rowe Ltd., Chippenham, Wiltshire

AND

In *Survive the Worst and Aim for the Best*, Kerry Katona shows how she has used some of her worst experiences to learn positive life lessons. Through her own experience, Kerry shows us how:

- your past doesn't have to be your present
- only you can help yourself
- to be proud of who you are, despite what others may say
- things may look different tomorrow
- not to judge others without knowing the full story

Above all, Kerry shows us that the struggle really *is* worth it. And that the things that really matter are often those closest to you.

3 4143 00729 0578

Contents

Introduction

I didn't make the most star-studded entrance into the world. My dad spent only a brief moment in my mum's life. He was already married and had a family, and he didn't want another one. My mum had already had it tough. Her own mother was a prostitute so she herself was very likely a mistake. She'd never really been looked after and loved, and now she had a baby of her own. There was no doubting that my mum loved me but because she hadn't had a decent start in life, she found it hard to look after me. So a lot of the time I looked after her. There we were bobbing along together, just trying to make the best of things, but it wasn't always easy. Mum suffered from manic depression and sometimes went on binges with drink and drugs. This meant I often didn't know what was happening from one day to the next. What mood would Mum be in? Would she even be around or had she disappeared for a few days? Would she be high and out of control or would she be the warm, funny Mum who could share jokes with me? I honestly never knew what I was going to get but somehow we managed. Looking back I'm sure that one of the reasons we made it through, despite everything, was that we wanted to survive. Sure, Mum tried to take her own life but that was more a cry for help than her not wanting to be alive.

We also moved around a lot. I never lived in one place for longer than three years. By the time I was eleven I'd been to seven different primary schools. At thirteen I was taken into care, staying with four sets of foster parents before Mum and I were finally reunited. The idea of having any sort of life or career was never really part of my big plan—I just wanted Mum and me to be happy and safe. Anything else was a bonus. Even today, love and security are the things I value most in my life.

That's not to say I didn't want more in life. I had my dreams and they usually involved me being on stage in front of an audience. When I was at school, if there was ever a chance for me to be up there dancing, singing or acting I'd be the first to put my hand up. Being able to express myself that way gave me an escape from my real life and it made me feel so alive.

So I was thrilled when I was 'discovered' and asked to join an all-girl band—Atomic Kitten. That led to fame, money and a whole exciting new life, but it wasn't the end of my problems. I got married and divorced in a very public way, suffered from depression and battled with drugs. I've also had two little girls who I love and adore, and have another child on the way. So far it's been a hard, weird, sad, fantastic, crazy time. What it hasn't been is perfect, because nothing is. That's something I've learned. No matter who you are or what you have, life won't go smoothly. And if you're famous the pain is ten times harder, it really is. What you have to keep in mind is that things don't always turn against you because of something you did, or some mistake you might have made. You can make what you think are the most sensible choices and it can still go wrong. That's just the way life is.

Accepting this fact and learning to accept myself has helped me cope with whatever happens. I'm still trying and I know that my struggles are not over. There will be times I will fall down but I also know I can pick myself up again. It might not be easy but I can and will do it. And you can too.

In this book I'm going to talk about some of the things I've been through in my life because I'm hoping it might help other people. I'm not silly enough to think I have the answers to your problems but sometimes I think it helps to know that someone else has been there. Being alone with your problems is very hard. So is not being able to talk about them. The more you pretend that everything's OK and keep it to yourself, the lower you will sink. I know because it took me a long time to admit when things were falling apart for me. It takes courage to admit you're not coping with life and that you're not the fun person your friends thought you were. I didn't want my friends to feel sorry for me. I don't want you to read this and feel sorry for me. And I certainly don't want you to feel sorry for yourself. What would make me feel really good is if you read this book and thought, 'Well if she can do it, so can I.'

Love
Kerry

CHAPTER ONE

Tomorrow is a fresh start

I was eight weeks old before my dad came to see me. Mum had popped into the pub for a quick one and was told that someone wanted to see her. My dad brought his brother and a friend along for moral support. They all came back to the house and crossed my palm with silver. That was the last time Mum and I saw my real dad. He went back to his wife and family. It wasn't the best start in life, but I've always tried not to look backwards and think about what might have been. To me it makes more sense to go forwards and try and make the best of what you have.

When I was still a toddler, Mum met a man who seemed to care a lot about her and they got married. For a while I had two parents and a childhood like a lot of other kids. I was living at home with my mum and dad, just like my friends did with theirs. I had no real idea of the troubles my parents were going through. I had toys, friends and went to school. What more could a little girl need? All of that changed in January 1987. Mum and Dad had been married for just over three years when he finally threw Mum out. I was just seven years old. From then on, for a lot of the time, my life was something I just did to survive.

You can't choose your parents and that means you can't choose a lot of what life deals out to you. I chose to try and lead as normal a life as possible, whatever that means. I am somebody who tries to be positive no matter what. I'm not sure where that comes from, but I figure that when they gave my family all the tough stuff, they thought they'd better give me a sense of humour and a way of bouncing back. Even in the darkest moments I've always felt life would get better—if not the next day, then the day after. That's what has always kept me going. Sometimes it really did get better but at other times it just got worse. Even then I refused to believe that things wouldn't turn around. I think part of the battle is not letting those doubts and fears really get to you.

It wasn't always easy. Life with Mum was shaped by her mood swings, a result of her manic depression. The low times would give way to periods when it seemed like she was flying and you never knew which Mum you were going to get. I just looked forward to the day when things would get better which they usually did. I learned to take pleasure in little things that we did. Mum and I have the same quick wit and we've always made each other laugh. Whatever problems we had at home (wherever home was) we still had good times together. If she had some spare cash she'd take me on the bus for a day out to Blackpool and we'd scream our way through the rides together. She was as much of a kid as me. I wished these moments would happen more often, but I tried to make the most of them and live from day to day. I think that living for the moment is one of the best ways of getting by when things are a bit tough.

I knew that not every child had a mother that would disappear, go on drinking binges or love a man who was very violent, but I always believed our life would get better. Part of being able to survive was not spending too much time thinking about it all. If I'd thought deeply about what my life was really like, I might never have made it through. Instead, I always felt there'd be something around the corner. I knew that sometimes I just had to go through hell to get there.

Maybe the fact that Mum couldn't

look after herself made me feel I had to be positive and strong. Like a lot of kids from troubled childhoods, I grew up pretty quickly and became the adult when I had to. I'd adapt myself to whatever was happening. I could charm the police if they'd been called. I could look after Mum when she self-harmed or had a panic attack. When she was down I'd cook her supper and give her a cuddle. But there were loads of times when it just seemed to be out of control. And then there were the suicide attempts. Every time she tried it, I'd feel guilty that I wasn't doing enough to make her want to stay alive. I was also confused because I didn't know what more I could do. Looking back I can see that Mum was crying out for help. Her depression made her believe she was a bad mother and that I'd be better off without her. But no matter what she did, I didn't want to be without her.

So it really broke my heart when

she decided at one point to give me up and live with her violent lover, Dave Wheat. Over the years, Dave had been in and out of Mum's life and I thought he was gone for good. When I was about twelve years old Mum and I were living in a hostel up north. Mum disappeared for a few days and then I heard she was with Dave in the East End of London. I didn't want to be with him, but I didn't want to be without her so I went to live with them. When things got violent with Dave (as they often did) and Social Services found out, Mum had to make a choice—Dave or me. She chose Dave. I went to stay with a foster family and just got on with it. Of course I thought about her, but what choice did I have? You can either sit there wishing things were different or you can just pull yourself together and be thankful for what you do have.

That's not to say I always had a smile on my face. Nobody can live like that. There were times I did have the sort of dark, negative feelings that can eat you up, thoughts of revenge, anger and sadness.

I remember on one occasion Dave, Mum and I had gone to The Three Rabbits for a drink. It was the sort of pub that gangsters hung around in; the sort of men who carried guns and knives and weren't afraid to use them. Dave had always scared me and he had the reputation to go with it. That night, when we left the pub and got into the car, Dave and Mum started arguing. He punched her and the argument stopped. It was soon to start again and this time it got really bad. By the time we got home and into the house, Dave had already kicked and punched Mum again. Now she was scared he would start coming for me, so she told me to run upstairs to my room and I did. But I could hear her downstairs, screaming. I came down to have a look and saw Mum with blood streaming from her leg. Dave was holding a knife. When he saw me, I thought I was done for. I went to him and put my arms around him, hugging him and telling him what a good day we'd all had. It was a tactic that had worked before and thankfully this was one of those times. I kept calming him until he relaxed. Then I took the knife from his hands and put it back in the kitchen. Eventually he fell asleep, and it was then that I thought about killing him. The only thing that stopped me was the thought that he might wake up and kill me instead.

I believe that staying positive was one of the reasons I was able to get away from my past and get the big breaks that came my way. Even now, I still try and take each day as it comes. That's even more important when you've got problems to deal with. It's so much easier to manage if you're only thinking about the next twenty-four hours instead of the next six months.

None of that stopped me having my dreams. As I've already said, as a little girl I loved to perform for family and friends. So when I got that lucky break and was invited to be the first member of Atomic Kitten (who were to become one of the most popular girl bands ever) you can imagine how I felt. That was an amazing change in my life—both good and bad. Fame can be great fun but it also has a downside. Until you've had your life exposed in public you've no idea how insecure you can feel. Nothing prepares you for that feeling. When Atomic Kitten started to get famous I found it more and more difficult to deal with strangers coming up to speak to me. Even worse is the way the press worms its way into your life. Becoming well known opened my eyes to the fact that nothing is without its price.

Bryan McFadden and his band

Westlife were already successful when I met him. Looking back it seemed like an almost too-perfect story. Girl from new girl band meets boy in popular boy band, falls in love and they get married. When it happened, I really felt that all my struggles had amounted to something. I thought I'd finally got the life I had always wanted. I'm not talking about the fame or the fancy houses; I mean the love and security that comes from having a family life. It didn't turn out that way. Our break-up was really hard because it wasn't just the end of a relationship; it was the end of my dream. Bryan had rejected me and was not going to change his mind. My depression got worse and I went through a real low. I'm still struggling with it—although it's not as extreme as Mum's, it's still pretty bad and can stop me in my tracks for long periods of time.

I know there will be times where I struggle more than others. Some days and weeks it's not easy at all. Will I ever leave the dark times behind? Maybe not. I also know my childhood means there are things that may always lurk in the shadows, waiting to come and get me when I'm feeling weak.

What makes me take heart and gives me strength is that I've managed to get through a lot of bad stuff already. I've done it by trying to take each day as it comes and not putting too much pressure on myself. If today turns out to be a bad day, then I look forward to tomorrow. I know that things will turn around and I just have to be patient. Nobody's life is ever going to be pain- and trouble-free, and it's worth keeping that in mind when you're feeling sorry for yourself. Believe me, tomorrow will be better. You have to hang on to that thought.

CHAPTER TWO

Even a girl from nowhere can get somewhere

Some people are born with silver spoons in their mouths. Others are lucky to get fed. I guess I'm somewhere in between. Let's be clear about this. In the big picture of life, I'm nothing special. I don't have a strong voice, but I can hold a tune. I'm not the prettiest girl around, but I know that I come to life and sparkle in front of the cameras. I haven't had a great education, but I do have a quick sense of humour and am pretty good with comeback lines. I wasn't trained for anything much, but I will work hard and I am a fast learner. If anything I've proved that you don't have to come from a 'good' background, know the right people or be a super-beautiful, tall, skinny babe to make it in this world. What you have to do is grab your moment, work as hard as you can and never give up.

There was really nothing in my life to suggest that I would end up being part of a successful pop band like Atomic Kitten, live in a lovely house with two wonderful little girls or be offered loads of new opportunities on TV and even a film. It's all miles away from where I began. I mean, a girl whose mum has a mental illness and who is always being moved around between foster families and schools every few years can't amount to much, can she? It's funny, but even though I didn't come from the best of backgrounds I never thought for one moment that I was worth less than other people. I always felt I had a place in the world, even if it wasn't the most secure place. And I didn't waste time looking at what other people had. I just thought about me.

It wasn't always easy because I

spent a lot of time looking after my mum. She would be high on drink or drugs or going through one of her manic moods. I'd just have to try and remain calm and be there for her. I think she knew it was hard for me but she just couldn't help herself. Listening to her after one of her suicide attempts was the worst. She'd sit there saying how sorry she was, how she was a bad mother and how she should be dead. It was so hard to make her feel better so I stayed in my room, out of the way. I felt guilty that I couldn't help her and I didn't want to make things worse.

Trying to believe there was something better wasn't always easy. I remember often being left alone when my mum was out. I just looked after myself, eating tomato ketchup sandwiches, watching TV and going to bed when I got tired. I was OK until it got dark when all the videos I'd watched got to me. Then I'd imagine there were ghosts everywhere and I had to hide in bed because I was so scared. I think I knew deep down that life could be better than this. I just didn't know what it could be. After all, who did I have to show me a better way?

I'll be honest. My mum didn't exactly make it easy for me to get ahead. She let me down time and time again but I refuse to blame her for anything. I don't think that's fair and it's just too easy to use other people as an excuse. After all, loads of people have problems in their lives. I know she wasn't the best parent in the world but I could always talk to her. In her own way she loved me. She's a great friend—a better friend than a mother. She's always listened to me and never allowed anyone to slag me off. She always did her best to be supportive and she still is. She was never like any of my mates' mums, and she never tried to be, but she was still my mum. Despite all our problems, I accepted her and loved her.

Looking back, I think that my ability to face difficulties and work through them has really helped me get on. I'm not one to spend my time asking, 'Why me?' and 'Why can't bad things happen to other people for once?' The thought might pass through my head but I don't let it stay there. People ask me how I managed to cope. I guess I didn't think of it as coping. I just thought of it as the life I was living. With all the moving around, the different 'parents' and no real home, I knew it wasn't the best life. But when you're in it, you don't see it like people on the outside do. It's your life and it's the only one you've got so you have to make it work. If you think about it, there are loads of situations that you just have to deal with. It's like those times you're forced to work with someone you don't like. We can't choose everything in our lives, but we can choose not to make it harder than it is.

I suppose I am pretty determined by nature and maybe my background made me even more so. I got a job as soon as I could. I'd seen Mum with nothing and I knew I didn't want to end up the same. I was only fourteen but I wanted my own money and my freedom, and I've worked ever since to make sure I've always had them. My first job was working in a shoe store in Warrington on Saturdays and in the summer holidays. While I was there I was offered a job collecting glasses at the World, one of Warrington's nightclubs. I was sacked after two weeks because they found out I was too young. I also worked at JD Sports. I'll always remember the day Mel C from the Spice Girls came in with her brother. We were all doing our best to be the ones who served them. After they'd gone we spent ages rewinding the CCTV recordings to look at her and then looking at her signature on the

23

receipt!

I eventually managed to get through my GCSEs and began a sixth-form course in Leisure and Tourism. At sixteen I knew it wasn't what I wanted to do with the rest of my life. I also knew I didn't have the ability to pay attention to the lessons. What I did have was a 34DD chest and a size 6 waist. I decided the way forward was to become a Page-Three Model. I'd seen how successful many girls had become. And so I had some pictures taken and sent off to the *Sun*, who phoned up and told me to come to London. I was on my way!

The shoot was to be with Beverley Goodway, a very well-known glamour photographer. Of course I thought Beverley was going to be a woman, so it was a surprise when 'she' turned out to be a man. He was very friendly and made us feel at home. All around the studio were pictures of the big name glamour girls: Linda Lusardi, Melinda

Messenger and Sam Fox. Now I wanted my picture up there as well.

I posed in a thong against these backdrops that made it look like I was on a beautiful beach somewhere! The funny thing was that, because I'm so short, I was standing on a pile of phone books—these are the things you never see! Anyway it all went well and I went home.

The only problem was that I'd got excited and told my teachers, and they'd told Social Services. That was it. Social Services stopped it because it would have looked really bad for a girl in care to be on Page Three! This made me start to think about trying to get my own flat. I wanted to be able to decide things for myself. In a way I've always done that—I've had to—and, though hard, it has given me good life skills. You have to look at things from all sides. Even though my childhood was not carefree, at least I learned to make decisions for myself as well as for my mum. As it turned out, that wasn't bad training for the life as a performer that I was about to have.

I never planned to be in a band but I had always been a bit of a show-off and, as I've said, I loved to perform for family and friends as a kid. One night, I'm out there doing my Kerry thing on the dance floor in a nightclub called Mr Smiths when it happens. My first big break! I had on long white pants and a bra top with ties that wrapped around my bust and revealed quite a lot of my boobs. The music was pumping, the place was hot and sweaty, and I was dancing and showing off when a guy comes up and asks me to audition for a band.

It was actually a dance band called the Porn Kings (no, it wasn't rude) and they wanted dancers to go with them on tour. They asked me if I had a passport, because they were going to appear at a big awards ceremony in Berlin. I was nervous and scared, but with Mum's support I decided to go. I think she knew that this was a major moment for me. I reckon everyone has their moment in life, but some people miss it because they're not ready or are looking for something else. Others just grab it and make the most of it. That's me. Through one of the guys I'd met, I was introduced to another guy who was putting a band together. And that's how, in 1999, I became the first member of Atomic Kitten, who became one of the most popular girl bands.

Atomic Kitten was a blast. I've never known a buzz like the one you get out on stage with the crowd cheering for you. The biggest thrill I got was when I made contact with people in the audience. I remember once catching the eye of this gorgeous little girl who was in her daddy's arms. She looked up at me and I looked back and blew her a kiss. The smile she gave lit up her

27

face and made me feel amazing. That's what it's all about.

And of course there was the lifestyle that went with it. Sometimes I'd lie awake at night in some posh hotel room and feel like pinching myself. I'd think about how far I'd come since the days when Mum and I had moved around Manchester, staying in refuges. We had no idea what the next day had in store for us.

By the summer of 1999 it was all taking off big time and, boy, was it mad! After a week in the recording studio, we might be appearing live on *SM:tv*. Then we would have to change our clothes and do another TV show, *CDUK*. Next we'd get back in the van and drive to Birmingham to do a gig at the uni. After that a college gig in Manchester, before boarding a private jet back to London to sing for Children in Need. There were times when we'd appear at between three and five schools a day. I loved it because the kids were so excited to see us. One time we even did a gig at my old school, Padgate High. How I'd made it from my childhood to here was pretty amazing.

I can honestly say I've never been driven by fame. Having said that, though, I did have a sixth sense that it would happen to me one day. Even so it has never been the most important thing to me. I had always wanted a job so that I could look after myself. I didn't want to ever be on the dole with nowhere to live. I'd been there with Mum and that was enough. I also knew I craved love and respect from other people and that I wanted the sense of security and self-worth a job would give me.

Maybe that's why I went on the television show, *I'm a Celebrity . . . Get Me Out of Here!* The idea was that I'd join a bunch of celebrities in the Australian jungle to see who could survive the longest. I'd said yes originally because I knew I could raise a lot of money for my chosen charities. But perhaps there was something in me that wanted to show the world I could step out of my comfort zone. And believe me I was way out of any comfort zone. I hated those early days in the jungle. I was scared. I had panic attacks and I whinged all the time. As the days went by I got into it. Somehow, when it came to the final day, I was still there and I won. That was a big deal for me. I know it's only a TV show but the experience was huge. It made me realise I could do anything I wanted—if I set my mind to it. It's a lesson I've held on to.

Of course it hasn't always gone smoothly. The pressures of work and maybe years of just pretending it was OK took their toll. I spent six weeks in a clinic in Arizona. It was the first time I had ever talked openly about my past—and faced it. I looked back and talked about how I felt about Mum's suicide attempts and the decisions she made about me. A whole lot of awful things came tumbling out but it helped me set a path for the future. There are people who've had tougher lives than me who've gone a lot further than I have. There are also people who had better chances and ended up flushing their lives down the toilet. I know I'm still young and there is a lot that could still happen, but I will do my best to make sure that I keep it together. After all, it's taken a lot of effort to get there.

CHAPTER THREE

Accepting people as they come

On 29 October 1960 in a dark back alley in Warrington, an eight-month-old baby girl was found wrapped up in blankets in a pram. Her mother was a prostitute who'd left her while she went to work. At least that's the story Mum always told about her beginnings. The truth was, her mother was a prostitute but she had left the baby with a friend while she went to work. When she didn't come back the friend called the police. The baby was then taken to the police station and admitted to the National Children's Home in nearby Frodsham. That was the start Mum had in life. From there it just got harder for her. Most people who meet my mum will never ever know anything about her. But they'll still judge her. Just like people judge me. We all do it. A lot of the time we're trying to make ourselves feel more important or special. At the end of the day I don't think it does make you feel any better—you just end up wasting energy on things that really shouldn't matter.

It's just too easy to look at other people and pass judgement. The truth is that we don't really know anything about most of the people we talk about. For example, my mum can be crude, rude, loud and a bit scary. She can also be loving, warm, kind, sweet and helpful—but lots of people won't know that. During my childhood I watched people form their opinions of her and judge her. They didn't understand her background or her life. They just saw what they saw. Seeing how cruel people can be has made me more aware of not doing the same thing myself.

Mum was eventually fostered, but

her real mum didn't make it easy for her to get on with her life. She would come around to where Mum lived and shout and threaten to smash things up. Of course, she was too young to remember any of this but her Social Services record shows that it had an effect on her. It said she had real doubts about her identity. Imagine feeling like that at such a young age. At four years old she was put into Statham Avenue children's home in Warrington because Social Services felt it would be more secure. It may have been secure, but it was not a happy place for a little girl. In fact the discipline they used would be seen as well over the top these days.

Once at the home, a girl called Julie pushed in front of Mum in the morning queue for a wash and cod liver oil. Mum gave her a shove out of the way and was bitten on the hand by Julie's sister. You had to look after yourself in there so Mum did what I reckon many of us would have done on instinct—she bit the girl that pushed her. The woman who was in charge—and I still can't believe this—bit Mum on the ear. This was the woman who was supposed to be looking after her! After that, Mum had to stay in the corner of the playroom all day, even when she wet herself. Once, when she refused to eat her rice pudding, her nose was held while they forced spoonfuls into her mouth. Of course she threw up all over the place. She was then slapped and sent to bed.

She must have been pretty tough to survive that place. I know it has left her with lots of mental scars. Even now, in her mid-forties, she has to have the TV on for company as she goes to sleep. Mum never had stability. She never had the security of knowing who was looking after her when she was a child because it always changed. So her views of life were shaped by that. Just when she thought she had some stability, her life would be turned upside-down in the worst possible way. She had no money and no family to turn to when she needed support. She's been the victim of domestic violence by both her real father and a lover. She's had to deal with the darkness of depression. Being involved in a serious car accident when she was eighteen can't have helped. She was thrown through the windscreen, leaving her face and head badly cut. A piece of glass was lodged in her head, giving her terrible headaches until it was found by doctors many months later. It's hard to tell whether the accident increased Mum's mental problems, but after the crash she began to have major mood swings— and continued to do so. Of course when I was a child, I didn't understand about manic depression and what it can do to people. I used to think she was mad sometimes. Now, having battled depression myself, I have a better understanding of why she was that way and why it was so hard for her to control herself.

Mum had it hard in ways most people would never know. When I think back now about things that she did—like choosing to have me fostered so she could stay with her violent lover—I realise that in many ways she didn't have a choice. From the time she was abandoned as a baby she has had to fight to survive. She has never felt loved or secure for long enough to build a life. So the idea of making a life for someone else must've been quite hard for her.

Meanwhile she certainly gave people a lot to talk about. When she was twenty-seven, she had a lesbian affair. I say 'affair' but it was clear that Mum and her lover, Tina, cared about each other a lot. If that was going to make Mum happy, it was fine by me. Other people were not so open-minded. On my ninth birthday,

Mum and Tina let me invite ten friends to my party. We waited and waited for them to show up. But no one came—because the other parents didn't like my mum being a lesbian. If she wanted to be loved in that way it was her choice. It was fine by me and it should have been fine with others. What I hated was the way people judged her, and then judged me because my mum was in a lesbian relationship.

As with all of us, Mum's life has shaped her and the way she behaves. It means that she does things that other people don't expect a mum to do. I mean, how many parents give their kids speed? It happened one night when I went to the toilet in a pub and found Mum and her lover Tina in there with some white powder. Mum told me it was sherbet. It tasted disgusting but it made me feel very confident. After that, doing speed with my mum became a regular thing at weekends. I felt guilty about taking it, because I knew it was wrong. Even then I knew I was letting myself down. On the other hand, my mum had given it to me so perhaps it couldn't have been that bad?

I'm not going to excuse her except to say that Mum and I did not have a normal mother-daughter relationship. We didn't have a normal life. While I think it's good to be friends with your mum, there have to be limits.

There were times when being around her could be a bit scary for someone from outside our circle. When I introduced her to Bryan McFadden for the first time, we all went to our local pub for a drink. Mum was pretty cool about meeting a guy from Westlife, one of the hottest bands around. But that was never going to be the problem. One of the girls in the pub got jealous of the way her husband was talking to Mum and her mates, and started making trouble. When Mum didn't react, the girl started in on her mate. Before we knew it, a fight had kicked off and they all got involved. In the end the girl who had started it got a good hiding and left. I'll be honest and say it did embarrass me in a big way. I tried to play it down with Bryan. 'Oh, it's just another Saturday night. It's fine, Bryan. You'll get used to it if you stick around.' Deep down I was sure Bryan would never want to see me again. To his credit, he took it all in his stride. I guess that's one of the qualities that I liked about him. After all, if someone accepts your family that's a good start.

I'll admit there have been times when I've been worried about how Mum might behave. When everything took off with Atomic Kitten, she was over the moon and really got caught up with all the excitement. She came to our gigs and would save all the bits that were written about us in the papers. I always worried that she would get pissed and let me down. I knew that Mum would never be anything but herself, but all the same I didn't want to feel like an idiot in front of the new people I'd met. But I needn't have worried. She was mostly fine. As for the odd occasions, well, everyone has those, don't they?

Of course, I've since had to go through the hell of having people judge me. There have been some truly awful times. While I was pregnant with my first baby I was staying with my mum. I received a hand-delivered, hand-written letter calling me every name under the sun. It said I would be a terrible mother and that the baby should be aborted. I have no idea who I could have hurt so much that they would want to write such nasty things. Most people know that I'm a good person who would do anything to help anyone. I was only a human being, carrying a baby, trying to do my best.

I have to say, Mum really helped when I had my first baby, Molly. Like a lot of new mums I was anxious, and at times I was probably over the top. I used to imagine all the bad things that would happen to her. What if she stopped breathing? If she slept too soundly, I'd gently prod her to make sure she was still alive. All my fears made me really upset, and I'd tell Mum that I was going insane. 'It's OK, Kerry,' she said calmly. 'Every mother's like that with their first child.'

Being well known means that you are always being judged on how you look, what you wear, how you act, what you eat, who you go out with, what house you live in—nothing is out of bounds. There are so many magazines that are just devoted to gossip. And mostly that's exactly what it is, just gossip. I guess that the public feel they know me and other people who are 'on the telly'. While I do give my fair share of interviews, most of the stories you read in these magazines have not come from me. They're bits that have been put together from rumours and second-hand information. Sometimes they print pictures that are three months old or even older! It really annoys me when it happens, because I know most of it is just not true but people are going to have an opinion about me because of it. You know what I mean—stuff like I might have had a small disagreement with my boyfriend at the supermarket and they'll turn it into a headline. 'Kerry goes bonkers.' That's bad enough. But what really gets me is when people write lies and everyone thinks they are true. I don't think being in the public eye means that you should be a target for people who are simply bitter and nasty.

Going out and not having a drink, in case you're labelled an alcoholic, is really annoying. These days, when I go to the toilet, I never take my bag with me. I'm also careful not to sniff when I come out, in case I'm labelled a drug addict! Even so they'll still find something to write about me. Well, I am human. I go to the shop in my sweatpants. I don't wear make-up or wash my hair every day. I get grumpy, tired and miserable. I put on weight. I lose weight. I make the wrong decisions. I also love my family, am loyal and kind, would do anything for my friends and know how to crack a good joke.

I know that putting someone down is something we all do to make ourselves feel better and less insecure about our own failings. But you know what? It just makes you feel worse about yourself and you end up in a really negative state of mind. For me it's more important to just try and get on with my life—and to be Kerry. If people like me, that's great. If they don't, then I don't care. I am who I am and I'm not going to change. And, if they think that spending time pointing out where I've gone wrong (or my mum has, or anyone else), then that's their problem. The way I see it, it's just a waste of energy that you could be using to improve yourself and your own life. And that makes a whole lot more sense to me.

CHAPTER FOUR

Learning from the hard times

By the time I was thirteen I'd been to eight schools. I'd whizzed through them all like an express train. When I tell people, they wonder how I managed to adjust. As they point out, it's bad enough trying to fit into one school! The truth is that it became a great escape from my home life. I loved art, drama and music. Whenever we put on a show at school I was up there, singing and dancing. I also found it easy to make friends and would settle in very quickly, no matter where we moved. Though moving around might have stopped me from having a stable childhood, it also meant I learned a lot about life, about myself and other people. I've heard it said that you learn more about yourself during the hard times, and I think that is true. I really think that you can come out of it as a stronger person. And maybe even a better one.

Social Services once reported that I was a kid who always 'bounced back'. That's very nice of them, but I have to ask what choice do you have? I mean, if you don't bounce back then you're done for. As I see it everyone has their trials in life. Provided we're healthy, most of us have two choices. Let it destroy you. Or go with it and believe that life can and will get better. Looking back at my childhood, I realise that I have always tried to find something positive in my life. I think part of that is because it's just the way I am, which is a lucky thing. It's also something I've tried to do as I've got older, because it actually stops you being miserable.

One thing I learned was that, however bad my life was, there were many others who had problems that were worse. Going to stay in a women's refuge with Mum was something that really opened my eyes. It was full of women of all ages and nationalities, and from many walks of life. There were prostitutes, addicts and people just like us. All of us were homeless because we'd had to escape from someone who was violent, threatening or abusive. Everyone had a story to tell and I met some of the loveliest women you could ever meet. Hearing them made us both feel a little better about our own situation, and made us realise that we were not alone. I remember an Indian woman who was there with her beautiful little daughter. Her husband had sexually abused the little girl before pouring a kettle of boiling water over her private parts. She would be damaged forever.

As part of the refuge's aftercare service we got taken on our very first holiday. I was so excited. I knew that proper families went on holiday to all sorts of places, sometimes abroad. Mum and I had never been anywhere. They sent us to Pontins holiday camp with some other people from the refuge for a whole week. I'd never been anywhere like it. Mum and I had our own apartment. I entered all the singing and dancing competitions and won the lot. We had the most fantastic time ever, and there was nothing to remind us of what we'd left behind. Mum was relaxed and happy. As for me, I was so happy that I could just be a carefree kid for a change.

As you can imagine, because of our moving around, I didn't make many lasting friends. I just learned to get on with the kids I was with for however long I was with them. If my schooling suffered I wasn't aware. Maybe I didn't learn a lot about maths, geography and literature, but I still learned things that would set me up for the future. I love meeting new people and making new friends.

That's something I've had to do from the word go, so I find it easy. The fact that we never stayed long in one place was also the ideal training for being in a band and going on tour. Don't get me wrong—I'm not saying that school is worthless. I'm proud that I managed to get my GCSEs. I regard the schooling of my own girls as one of the most important things I can do for them. I want them to do as well as they possibly can. They have an option I didn't have.

Thinking back now, I learned about life in so many different ways. Being the 'grown-up' one in my relationship with Mum meant that I also handled the money when we lived together. Mum would sign the income support book and I'd go and cash it. I'd give Mum her spending money and hide the rest so we'd have enough for the shopping. I was quite a good money manager. I went out and bought what I needed when I needed it. I mostly lived off tomato ketchup butties. The only thing I often bought for myself was a Dime bar. I tried to make sure that when Mum was home there was always something for her to eat.

Mum and I lived in some rough areas, but some were worse than others. Early on I found out that you had to stick up for yourself. There was a field at the back of our block where I often played with our Jack Russell terrier, Pip. Mum would watch me from the kitchen window. All the kids played there and someone had hung a rope and an old tyre from a tree to make a swing. One day a girl pushed me off it. She refused to let me have another turn so I ran home crying. All Mum could say was, 'I'm going to smack you if you don't go outside right now, push her off and get back on the swing yourself.' I wasn't really thinking as I went back outside and actually head-butted the girl. I'll never forget that sound. As soon as I did it I felt really bad and realised it wasn't the right thing to do. Afterwards I went round to her house and apologised to her mum.

The thing I longed for most is the one thing that most people probably say they hate—the ordinary stuff of life. I wanted a routine with parents who went to work and came home. I loved the idea of a real home and friends who would come and stay. I wished that my mum was like a normal parent. I thought that, if we could escape from the life we had, Mum would never attempt suicide again. Instead, I tried to find my own ways of escaping. When we lived for a time on the Romford Road with Dave, Mum and he would go to the pub. I would nip home to watch videos. My favourite was *The Jacksons: An American Dream*. It was the story of the Jackson family and how the boys turned to music and formed the Jackson 5 to escape their violent father. That really rang a bell with me.

Later on, when I was at high school, my friend Lisa and her mates used to make me stand in the middle of a circle so I could sing Michael Jackson songs and moonwalk for them. I'm sure that my desire to perform comes out of that need for escapism. If you can't run away from your actual life, the one thing you can do is act out a different one. It seems that my need to find that other life was a major reason behind my being picked as the first member of Atomic Kitten. It wasn't my voice, because compared to the other girls I wasn't a good singer. I've since been told that what made them pick me was the fact they knew instantly I was going to be a star, and that I'd bang my head against a brick wall until I got there. They called it the Marilyn Monroe Syndrome. They reckon that I had the same huge desire as Monroe did to leave the past behind.

Escaping into my fantasy world was

one way of coping. The other way I dealt with bad times was to think about what else was going in the world. When I was put with my first foster family they weren't very nice to me. That was actually the first time in my life I felt so low I wanted to kill myself. I stopped feeling sorry for myself when I looked through one of my foster mum's magazines. It was full of real-life stories about awful things that people had been through. One story was about a kid around my age who had been kept locked in a cupboard and fed only on bread and scraps. Twice a day she was allowed out—so her father could abuse her. When I read that and some other nasty stories it made me think I was lucky. I had a mum who loved me, and one day things would change and I would be back with her. I didn't have it that bad.

There are many people—people who've had far more success than me—who've had really tough lives but they never let it stop them. I've often thought that, maybe, what helped them get there is learning early on that success in life doesn't always come easily. And they never moaned about it. If you take the attitude that it's quite normal to have to work and, yes, even struggle for what you want, then the idea of bouncing back after a setback will seem more reasonable. Instead of seeing the tough times as something that shouldn't happen, you look at them as part of the journey. Would I have been Kerry if I hadn't come from where I did? Would I have even developed the imagination I have and my deep love of life? Would I have had the guts to take the chances when they came? I'm not sure. When your journey gets a bit too rocky, just remember—one day you will look back on it and think that it helped make you who you are.

CHAPTER FIVE

Love and security, the two most important things

I don't know what it was that Bryan McFadden saw in me. Perhaps he fell in love with me because I made him laugh. I know that I loved him because he made me laugh. He also made me feel wanted and safe. I had never felt like that before. When he asked me to marry him I saw it as my chance to have the family life I had dreamed of, and now I thought I was going to have it. I could see it all. I'd have a great big loving family with Bryan by my side. Love and security are still more important to me than anything—money and fame do not come close. You can be happy almost anywhere if you feel safe and loved.

Of course, money does make you a bit more secure, but there are loads of people who grow up with money who are very insecure. So it doesn't always help. I want my kids to feel secure about who they are. I want them to be confident without having to use alcohol or drugs and that means giving them a lot more than money. I want them to be truly happy and know what life in a family is really like. I want them to feel that if they want to take on the world they can. Most of all I want them to have a carefree childhood—the one I never had.

I'd never met anyone as romantic and caring as Bryan. We had the same sense of humour and were always coming up with one-liners that cracked us both up. I just fell head-over-heels, madly in love with him. People would pick him out as the 'ugly one' or the 'fat one' in Westlife, but to me he was beautiful. I wasn't interested in what he looked like. None of my boyfriends have followed a particular 'type', and I've always gone for the way they treated me. Being looked after is what matters most to me; it's what makes me feel secure. When Bryan told me our marriage was over I was utterly heartbroken, but my main worries were for the kids. I guess my nesting instinct kicked in.

I wanted to give them a good home and a stable routine, so I found a school and enrolled them straight away. I felt really lucky to have enough money of my own to be able to buy us a house. I was able to put Molly and Lilly in school and not have to move them around. They were not going to have a childhood like mine, I was 100 per cent sure of that. I know there are lots of people out there—maybe you're among them—who have been through tough childhoods. I think that for those of us who have managed to come through it all, there is a big need to make sure that the past never comes back into our lives. So maybe we try a bit extra with our kids. Maybe we go over the top? All parents want the best for their kids, but sometimes I wonder if I worry too much. I want things to be so perfect that maybe I try a bit too hard to control our lives.

Back when Mum had me, she probably thought about the same things. Just as I have hopes and dreams for Molly and Lilly, I am sure she must have had them for me. Things might not have worked out the way she wanted them to, but at least we made it through together. Many families don't even manage that. When I was pregnant with my first daughter, Molly, I thought a lot about my own life. Mostly I couldn't stop thinking about my real dad who I've never known. What would I tell Molly when she grew up? How would I tell her about my childhood? In spite of all that, I chose not to contact my real dad. Mum had told me his name and that he came from Liverpool. If I'd wanted to, I could

59

have found him but I chose to respect his decision to stick by his family. I comfort myself with the thought that perhaps he's seen me in the papers and knows who I am. Maybe he even feels proud of me?

One of the hardest things for me after having Molly was that, as much as I loved her, I missed working. One moment you can't believe you have this beautiful creature snuggled up in your arms and the next you're thinking about going to work and leaving her behind in the care of somebody else. I'll admit I did miss being part of things. Being able to perform is something that makes me feel proud of myself and we all need to feel that. Self-esteem is very important and I know a lot of new mums lose it very quickly. They feel fat, ugly and like they're not part of their old world any more. It's as if it's all been taken away. Even if you have got a husband who earns enough money, it's not just about that. In my work I have a lot of fun and I meet some great people. Plus it's always new. One day I might be hosting a TV show, the next filming commercials. When Bryan and I split, I wanted the financial security for Molly and Lilly. It's important for me to know I have my own money and I can look after them with no help if I have to.

I really try to keep life as smooth and even as possible for the girls. However, like lots of men and women who've been divorced, I sometimes disagree with my ex. When Bryan doesn't phone the girls or turn up when they're expecting him, it makes me really angry. Once, a car arrived late at night to take them to visit him in London. Bryan was annoyed that I wouldn't let them go. I didn't want to get them out of bed in the middle of the night to go with a stranger on a long drive. I thought it was too much for a two-and four-year-old. Nor do I think it's wrong to insist they start the school term on the same day as everyone else, even if they have to cut short their holiday with him. I really want them to have a normal life and be the same as their friends. I don't want them to feel different like I did.

Building a more secure life also means giving Mum what she's never had. One of the things I was most proud of was when I used some of my Atomic Kitten earnings to buy her a small three-bedroom house in Warrington. The whole idea of 'home' really matters to me because I never knew what it was like to stay in one place for longer than three years. When Bryan and I moved into our first home in Ireland, I thought I was living in one of those American shows where everybody always loves each other no matter what and life is perfect. I was so blown away by things—the dishwasher, the big staircase and the huge kitchen. I couldn't believe this was my life. I told Mum I was going to do it all properly. I talked about getting a sewing machine and doing gardening and lots of other homely stuff. It was my fairytale.

Losing it all was a huge shock. I'm not talking about the house. I'm talking about the feeling of being wanted and loved. We'd had some difficult times during our marriage. The pressures of work—of both our jobs—meant we were often away from one another, so it put a strain on things. Looking back, I can see now that Bryan was slowly changing. He had been behaving in a different way towards me for a while. Still I wasn't prepared for the phone call when it came. He simply said, 'I don't love you any more.' I tried to hold myself together while I took his words in. I had to keep it together if only for the sake of my kids. I have three rules that I try my best to keep—never raise your voice, never argue and never cry in front of the kids. From experience I know how easily you can frighten and upset a child. Your parents are the ones who are meant to be in control. I couldn't stop the tears rolling down my face. Molly saw me and asked me what was wrong. There was no way I was going to tell her the truth. I didn't ever want her to be the adult like I'd had to be with my mum. I didn't want her to feel responsible. That would go against everything I was trying to build. I told her I had a headache.

I've tried to keep everything positive for the girls because they are very young. I don't think they need to be exposed to negative or worrying things at this point—well, not if I can help it. When they are older I'm sure we will talk about Bryan and me, but until then I don't want them to feel that something isn't right. After the break-up I left Ireland and moved back to the UK. I didn't see the point in staying there while my mum and friends were in

England. At moments like this you need to be among those who love you. I'm very grateful for my friends. Many of them I've known from when I was a kid. These people are the ones that matter to me. Sure I've rubbed shoulders with 'celebrities' and gone out with them, but they are not the people I spend my time with.

You might not believe me about not caring that much about the whole fame thing but, truly, to me a loving family life is much more important. I'll admit that it was loads of fun at the start with Atomic Kitten. It was also very new, and new things are always fun, aren't they? There were private jets, posh hotels and celebrity parties. The other girls in the band, Liz and Tash, and I really went for it in those early days. Part of the fun for me was the escapism—being one of the Kittens was like acting, and so, because I wasn't being myself, it was easy for me. We behaved as we wanted (when our strict tour manager, Helen Knox, wasn't watching . . .) and really lapped it all up—as a Kitten should! But, as anyone will tell you, the novelty does wear off and it becomes really hard work being in the public eye for a lot of the time. It all depends what you value most, and the sooner you work that one out the better, I reckon. Getting pregnant really showed me what mattered—and it wasn't being on the road with a band. It was family.

Since Bryan and I broke up, I've returned to Warrington. It might not be very glamorous, but it's the place I feel most secure and happy. It's the place I've chosen to give my girls the childhood I want them to have. At the moment, we live in a private development in the grounds of what was the old Winwick Hospital. Winwick was also the hospital that Mum spent a lot of time in years ago! Living there now is like living in Toy

Town and when I see the lovely houses and gardens it just makes me smile.

These days it's all about creating a good life for me and my children. I have my mum close by, I have my friends and I have my work. Though I now know you don't always marry Prince Charming and live happily ever after, I think I have finally found someone I can share the rest of my life with. We all want and need love and security, and so many of us girls fall into the trap of sitting around and waiting for someone else to come along and provide this for us. No matter how independent we are, we think someone else will make it better. Yes, it can be the icing on the cake to be looked after, but you owe it to yourself to create your own little place in the world where you can feel safe and happy. If someone comes along and wants to make it even cosier, then you're very lucky indeed!

CHAPTER SIX

Finding the strength to move on

When Bryan was in Westlife and I was in Atomic Kitten we had busy working lives, which meant always being on planes and heading different ways. We also had the added pressure of trying to keep our relationship quiet, at least for a while anyway. The reason for that was, as well as not being seen drinking or smoking, the management had strict rules that we shouldn't be dating. Our image had to be kept a certain way for our fans. While it was a career high for me, it was a lot to deal with personally. Bryan and I were always on the phone and, if you've ever had a distance relationship, you know how tiring that can be. Mum would call with her own problems and I was tired from working. Looking back now, I can see that I was in a pressure cooker that was going to burst at some point. I realise now that it was the beginning of my own battle with depression. It's one of the hardest things I've faced and I know I will probably have to deal with it for the rest of my life.

I spent so much of my childhood playing grown-up to Mum that I guess I wasn't really prepared to deal with my own crisis when it came. As a kid I'd handled some really tough situations and I suppose everyone thought I could manage. The weird bit is that I thought I could too. I was a time-bomb waiting to go off. Like a lot of people I just kept going until finally something made me crack. As often happens in life, it wasn't just one thing. It was a whole lot of things.

About the time Bryan and I got engaged, I began to get more and more tired. The thought of making yet another single and going on the road was steadily losing its appeal. Our schedule was insane, and I was also finding it hard to deal with what the papers said about me. One day, when we were rehearsing at Virgin, everything came to a head. My mum phoned and wanted me to do something about a newspaper story about her. It was wrong and she wanted them to take back what they'd said. There was so much pressure at work I had no energy left for her. It all got too much. I locked myself in the toilet and cried non-stop. The doctors told me I had depression and gave me anti-depressants. Bryan came and took me home to Mum's where I was supposed to have two weeks off to get better. Deep down I'd always had an idea of what was wrong, but I just didn't want to admit it. I also thought that if I took the pills, that would be telling the world I had a problem. So

I threw them away, which was not the smartest thing I've ever done.

Not long after that I decided to leave Atomic Kitten. My decision wasn't sudden. I was finding the travelling hard, and learning I was pregnant with Bryan's child made my mind up. Maybe it was just as well, because the record company told me they hadn't really wanted me in the band anyway. I felt so rejected, as if my whole time with the band had been a lie. Being with the Kittens had helped my confidence and made me feel wanted—a rare thing in my life. Suddenly all the good things I'd ever done with the band melted away. I guess my whole life has been built on shaky ground and it didn't take much to make everything fall apart. Maybe, if I'd had a more secure childhood, I would not have let it get to me as much as it did. With two small daughters now, I am very aware of building their self-esteem. If they can start from a strong place, they will find it easier to pick themselves up when they fall.

During the time I was with Bryan I thought he would always be there for me. I didn't imagine I would ever be alone again. I suppose part of that was wanting to make my dream of the perfect home life come true. And I was always wanting to know that other people were proud of me. I'm not saying there's anything wrong with that—it's great to have the approval of others—but now I think you have to make sure that you can get on in life without it. In other words, you have to be proud of yourself and look at anything else as a bonus. If you spend your life waiting for others to tell you how good you are, then it could be a long wait. And you can't build a life like that.

Breaking up with Bryan left me in pieces. The day he phoned and told me he wanted it to be over I refused to believe it. I kept phoning him back, begging him to change his mind, but he was having none of it. His mind was made up. Part of my shock wasn't just the news itself; it was also the way he could suddenly block me out. To be loved and then suddenly unloved is the emptiest feeling of all. Of course I did what we all do when a relationship ends—I thought all sorts of strange and bizarre thoughts. Had our relationship been a publicity stunt to help his singing career? Did he only come to meet me in Australia because I was the winner of *I'm a Celebrity* and this was a very high-profile thing for him? Maybe he thought he could make it without me now? Thoughts like these wouldn't go away and they were making me ill.

At first I tried to forget the pain by going out with my mates. My view was that I had to get on with life as normal, but that's so easy to say when you're still numb from the shock. Looking back, I can see I was falling apart slowly. I tried hard to keep positive which was a bit easier when the girls were with me. When they were away seeing their dad I just went backwards again. At my lowest point I even started taking drugs again, something I hadn't done for years. For those few hours, I didn't feel worthless or ugly. I didn't think about what I was doing to myself. I just wanted the pain to go away. There's little doubt that I was hiding from everything. I didn't want to see what was happening in my life, and I didn't want to admit I was at a really low point. As I slid down that slippery slope I blamed everyone except myself. The morning after a binge I'd be sitting there sobbing. Just as my mum did, I'd rake over the past, feeling even more sorry for myself. I would torture myself, wondering why people I'd got close to rejected me. But I wasn't ready to admit I had a problem. You can't solve the problem if you refuse to see it. That's what happened to me.

As many people know, meeting up with an ex is tricky stuff. You know how it is. You think you're ready to do it, but when the moment comes you're really not in good shape. One night, after meeting Bryan down in London, things really came to a head. I kept playing the details of our relationship over in my mind. I blamed myself, my upbringing and what it had done to me. Suddenly everything hit me and it was clear I wasn't coping. A couple of days later I found myself in the Priory, a well-known clinic. I needed a break from reality and the Priory gave me just that. It removed me from daily life and all the responsibility that came with it. Being there and having therapy sessions gave me a chance to stop and reflect—which was not something I had been able to do much in my life. I began to ask myself some hard questions. Slowly I realised that only I could help me.

Nobody else was going to do it. I was heartbroken about Bryan, but I still had two gorgeous little girls. I had to get my act together.

Knowing what you have to do and doing it are two different things. At least I had stopped trying to pretend I was OK. I think it's hard for a lot of people to admit they are not feeling as strong as they should. It's like you've failed and who wants to tell the world that? I was no different. I just wanted to keep playing 'good old laugh-a-minute Kerry', but the game had changed and so had the rules. Believe me, it's a big relief when you can admit to your friends that you are not coping. It's also very scary but, if they are your real friends, they will accept you.

I felt like a huge weight had been lifted from my shoulders, but the real struggle was yet to come. There was that first Christmas alone to get through, which proved to be a huge step. I tried hard to get into the spirit but all I wanted to do was hide under the duvet. It didn't help that Bryan had phoned on Christmas Eve to say he was dating the Australian singer, Delta Goodrem. I don't think I was ready for that, especially as Delta is such a beautiful girl. I certainly wasn't ready for all the arguments that were to happen about the kids and my career (Bryan thought I should stay home).

It wasn't long before I broke down again. This time a stay at the Priory wasn't enough. I had to get far, far away. My manager put me on the plane to Cottonwood Clinic in Arizona, where I would have more privacy than I'd have at the Priory and could really work it out. I arrived in Arizona on 4th July, American Independence Day. When I stepped off the plane, the heat smacked me in the face. The mixture of heat plus the alcohol I'd had on the plane meant I slept all the way to Cottonwood. When I arrived I was strip searched to make sure I hadn't hidden anything on me. They took away my CDs, deodorants, nail varnish, my copy of *OK!* magazine, bikinis, perfume, razors and tweezers. Because some of the patients were in for sex addiction, we were only allowed to wear modest skirts and tops. It was a pretty strict place but, as I found out, it was what I needed. Finally I could get my real feelings out in the open. It's very strange standing up in a group of people and saying, 'Hi, I'm Kerry. I'm a depressive.' Gradually I was able to admit I had problems with alcohol and drugs. I also had to confront my past. I read, I listened and I talked about myself. I also wrote things down. Things began to get clearer. For the first time I was able to admit that my childhood had affected my life as an adult. For the first time I understood that sticking by Mum and looking after her had made me feel wanted and useful, but at the same time it meant she kept acting the same old way. Finally I could stop pretending once and for all. I learned that the rejection I'd faced in my life played a huge part in the way I acted with others. After about a week I began to see that I couldn't do anything about the past. I had to let go and move on, one day at a time.

At the end of my four weeks at Cottonwood, I felt like a new woman. I was ready to try and find my place in the world again. I knew I still had work to do on myself, but I was ready. I had learned some important lessons, like when things go wrong it's easy to turn your anger and sadness on others. We all do it but it doesn't get us anywhere. It's just wasted energy. Instead of thinking about the boyfriend/ girlfriend that dumped you, you should spend your energy on healing yourself. That's what I learned and it makes really good sense. And you know what? Everything that happens isn't just about you. It's about the other person and what they have going on in their head and in their past as well. I'm not saying you can't get upset or feel anything. I just think that once you do the angry bit, you should try and put it behind you and get on with things. Holding on to the thing that hurt you is not going to help. Don't kid yourself that you're getting revenge on somebody by staying angry at them. The only person who will suffer is you.

Since my time in Cottonwood I've learned to take charge of my life and what happens to me. I've accepted that life has high and low moments. Things with Bryan aren't always easy. All I want is for us to share our children and for him to take an interest in their happiness. In the end I just want them to have a normal life. I know he loves his little girls. I hope that our relationship will improve as time goes on. I don't believe in bearing grudges.

I've also talked to Mum about the problems I had with her as a mother. At first she was hurt, but she did understand and since then she's really tried to be more of a mum to me. As for my depression, well, I take medication and it helps. I admit I long for the day when I can be the old me again—by that I mean more carefree. But I've also learned a lot about myself. In a way you have to go through the bad things to find out what's good. Don't be afraid if it happens to you. You're not a freak or a loony. You're just a person who has hit a nasty bump on life's journey.

CHAPTER SEVEN

Making myself proud

Flashback: I'm standing in the Australian jungle with a plastic crown on my head and a glass of champagne in my hand. I'm a mess and I stink but there are 16.7 million people watching me on TV. Everything is blurring in front of me. I won't take it all in until I get back to the real world.

Throughout my childhood I always wanted a proper family where we could all share in things together. As I grew up I longed to be a daddy's girl. I wanted to have a dad to laugh and share secrets with. I wanted him to be proud of me just like my mum is. Since then I've come to realise that I'm the one that has to believe in myself first of all. If I'm proud of

Kerry, then other people will see that and respond to me in a positive way. It's the same for all of us. If we show that we care about what we do and we commit to something, people will respect that. It could be a project at work, being part of a sports team or giving time to charity. But first you have to show that you are willing to put in the time and effort, and that you believe in what you're doing.

For me, appearing on *I'm a Celebrity . . . Get Me Out of Here!* was one of the biggest things I'd done. All of us have different reasons for wanting to do something. For example, there are loads of reasons why someone might want to be in a band. They might just love music. They might think they can do it better than other people out there. They might just be in it for the money or the fame. The big thing for me was always that sense of being able to say to myself, 'You did it, girl!' Everything I've done since

Atomic Kitten, whether it's acting, stage shows or television presenting, was as much about my need to be moving forwards as it was about earning my living. (And yes, I probably like showing off a bit too . . . !) 'Celebrity' was bigger than all of them in some ways, because it took me into a totally new place, not just physically but mentally as well. There are times in your life when you know you need to take a chance and this was one of them.

When I agreed to go on the series I had no idea what I'd let myself in for. I was up for a laugh. I also knew it would be worthwhile because of the charity aspect of the show. One of my chosen charities was the Temple Street Children's Hospital in Dublin where my daughter Molly was treated for suspected meningitis. The hospital staff were so good to us, and raising money to help them was the least I could do. I'd only seen bits of the first series, so I wasn't fully prepared for what was in store. Maybe that was just as well.

You can watch all the wildlife shows in the world, but nothing can prepare you for the Australian jungle. There might have been camera crews, and Ant and Dec hovering around as well, but that didn't change where we were. When I saw the patch of land that was to be our home for the next two weeks, I started to panic. We'd been told earlier about the dangerous insects, spiders and snakes we might meet. I started to imagine them hiding under every leaf and twig. Honestly, you can't help but imagine things when you're in a place like that. We were totally exposed to nature. There were just camp beds to sleep on with a bit of canvas over them to keep out the rain, but we still got wet. The 'toilet' was in another clearing. On the first night, I was woken up by another contestant, Neil 'Razor' Ruddock, whispering loudly, 'Snake!

Snake!' He wasn't joking. There really was a snake under my bed. My reaction was pretty pathetic. 'Oh God, please come and get me. I want to go home.'

In fact I was like that for a good few days. I did a lot of crying. I was tired from lack of sleep, missing the kids and not coping with the jungle at all. At one point one of the doctors on the show was rushed to see me because I was short of breath. It turned out I was having a panic attack. I started to feel like I'd let myself down. The only thing that kept me going was the thought of my mum. She would have been really cross with me if I didn't stay for the first week. As time went on I'd think of Mum, Bryan and my girls. I really wanted to make them proud and that kept me going. Katie Price helped me a lot as well. She was really kind and lovely. I also thought of the charities I was here to raise money for and said to myself, 'God, Kerry.

You've got a life of luxury at home. Two weeks in the jungle and you'll do a lot of good for other people. If you walk now, you'll be letting them down as well as yourself. Just get on with it.'

The belief that others have in me has always mattered. It's not just about the attention or them saying 'Good girl, Kerry' either. It's about me being able to repay their trust in me. Atomic Kitten gave me my very first chance to really apply myself to something and see what I could do. When they were putting the band together I was the first girl selected. At the time I didn't know if anything would come of it, but I did what I was asked. I went to singing lessons, and did all these boring voice exercises even though I hated them. I told myself that, if the band got off the ground, I wasn't going to be the one to let everyone down. When I wasn't singing I worked on our dance moves. I worked bloody hard, I can tell you.

I always try to learn from others around me and ask their advice. I think it shows that you are willing, and that you don't think you know everything (which, of course, nobody does). When I got the part in an Irish drama called *Showbands* I had never acted before. That meant people were taking a gamble on me. I counted myself lucky to be around a cast who helped and supported me. I was so scared and thought they'd think I was only in there because I was well known, but they were amazing and made me feel like one of the gang. That meant there was even more to live up to! I didn't want to let them down and I don't think I did. It's really important to me to be able to do what people expect me to do. It's not just that they're paying me. It's that I need to go to bed at night knowing I kept my side of the deal.

I haven't always managed it. Not

long after splitting with Bryan I had to go to Austria to film a TV show called *My Fair Kerry*. I'd committed myself to it before we broke up so I thought I'd better do it. The concept of the show was that I'd be staying with a wealthy, titled Austrian family who would turn me into a lady! I thought it might take my mind off all the stuff going on at home, but it didn't. As a result I messed it up. Count Carl-Philip Clam was my host. He was supposed to teach me how to walk, dance and speak proper, so I could mix with all the other posh Austrians. Because I was feeling so low anyway, it really hurt having him tell me that I didn't fit in and wasn't a lady at all. I really messed up that time and felt like a failure. For whatever reason, I wasn't able to give it my best shot and that's not something I'm pleased about.

One thing I was really proud of was winning Quality Street Celebrity Mum Of The Year. It was the second time in a row I'd won it and I was thrilled. I knew I was doing a good job giving my girls love and security, but it was great that other people thought so too! I received loads of cards and letters and I can tell you it really made me feel good. Of course, you should be able to feel proud of yourself without other people telling you all the time, and I think I've got better at that. I know that my childhood hasn't made it easy. Mum was too busy surviving to think about building her daughter's self-esteem. That's probably why I still get so stupidly excited whenever something does go well. Sometimes I just can't believe I've done it. That certainly happened with *I'm a Celebrity . . . Get Me Out of Here!* That was such a big deal for me.

Maybe there is part of me that wants to show people that I'm able to do things they don't expect. When Atomic Kitten got to Number Ten in the charts with the single 'Right

Now', I couldn't help thinking how fantastic it was that I'd made it despite everything. I just hoped those primary school teachers who'd written me off as trouble, just because I was under a council supervision order, would remember my name and see what I'd achieved.

What I want now more than anything is to get back to being the old, carefree me—the girl that went into the jungle. That means spending time on my career. I've got contracts with Iceland and *OK!* magazine, but I still love acting, singing and dancing so I'd love to get back into theatre, films or TV presenting. I'm proud to be involved with Pink Ladies—this is the private cab company that started in Warrington but now has branches in London, St Helens, Carlisle and Plymouth. Our whole aim is safety for women, so the drivers are all female and all passengers have to be account holders so no money changes hands.

As I write this I'm enjoying my relationship with Mark Croft and we are looking forward to the arrival of our baby. Mark is attentive and affectionate, and there's so much to look forward to in the future. And I'm still only twenty-six, so with any luck there are even more exciting things to come. I expect I will have some struggles sometimes but, let's face it, who doesn't? The difference for me is that I have to deal with them in the public eye and that is sometimes the hardest part.

At the same time I know that it's not just about me any more. I now have a duty to my two little girls, and also to my baby when he or she is born, to give them the self-belief they need to go ahead and try things. It means a lot to me to be able to give them chances in life that I never had. They will have an easier life than I did, that's for sure, but that doesn't mean they won't have to put in the effort. I don't want them to be the sort of kids that just try something for a while and then give up. I hope they will learn a few things from their dear old mum. I also hope they won't mind when their proud mum claps and cheers louder than all the rest.